How to remember your dreams

Amr Ezzat

How to remember your dreams

As a labyrinth
What do we remember from a labyrinth?   07

As companionship
As though God were with us   23

As prophecy
I see myself slaughtering you   35

As a walk
A journey to the marble desert   49

As enchantment
A meeting with nonexistence   65

As a battle
What we could suffer   79

As a blank space
Who draws all this nothingness?   91

Indexes   113

As a labyrinth
What do we remember
from a labyrinth?

For several mornings in a row I sat at the low kitchen table, my chin nearly grazing its surface, drinking the tea with milk that my mother made for me. I concealed my anger and fear; how could she have left me that night to get lost in the alleys of Imbaba?

Finally one morning a rebuke slipped from me. Struggling to hold back the tears flooding my eyes, I asked how she could have left me. Laughing, my mother cupped my cheek in her palm, saying nothing of the sort had ever happened, and never would.

Bursting into tears I retorted that I remembered it well, although I didn't recall that she'd returned and found me. Surely she had, for how else could I have made it home?

In pained surprise she looked into my eyes and stopped laughing. Wiping away my tears, she apologized profusely.

She was there, at a distance I felt unsafe for a boy who still doesn't know his way alone through the twisting alleys around my grandmother's house.

We were on our way there, and as she approached an intersection, she looked back to see me farther away than usual. She didn't call for me to draw near; she didn't wait for me. Her eyes simply met my own terrified eyes, and then she disappeared around the corner.

I sped to the corner and once there, I didn't find her. I ran to the next intersection, looked left and right, and didn't find her. I froze in place, and began sobbing bitterly.

I was lost. Where should I place that catastrophic incident with its foggy beginning and missing end? It repeated itself in various forms, with me getting lost in the club, near my school, in the market when I lost hold of my mother's hand, around our house when the familiar streets would not lead to ours.

This was not the only incident that took place; it was one of many exceptional incidents disconnected from otherwise ordinary events. The people I shared these experiences with had no awareness of them, or perhaps failed to remember what I recalled so well. When I recounted these exceptional incidents, they seemed to surprise my companions, and I was surprised to find them smile and heartily laugh. They'd empathize with me, and tenderly commiserate, then ultimately assert that the incident had never taken place. It was as though I had gotten a little lost in a place they knew well, and yet with all confidence they'd deny the event that had taken place there.

After being lost in a labyrinth—an experience that dissipates bit by bit—children gradually enter the world of reality holding tight to the hands of adults, confident in their ability to distinguish what truly happens from what doesn't. Adults differentiate between "reality" and between lies, imagination, dreams and fancies; between the connections, relations and conditions that govern true events and the others found in picture books, make-believe tales, and films.

Adults create stories and imaginary characters for the amusement of children, but if children believe them more sincerely than required for their childish amusement, or if they try to connect with the imaginary world or to summon it to the real world—for example by asking "why aren't there dragons at the zoo?"—adults are then obliged to deny the reality of it all.

Adults push children into constructed labyrinths of imagination, and then snatch them out at the appropriate time. Yet despite the confidence with which adults guard children from falling astray, their extrication from the world of imagination is not always convincing or final. The process of departure only grows convincing with time, as children join the world of adults and test out the labyrinth of life amongst strangers without a hand guiding them at every step towards safety. It comes with fumbling through experiences, until children grow accustomed to the networks of relations and conditions that govern the life of mature adults. It is in confrontation with this bewilderment that children learn the necessity of conceding to adults' conditions, so as to avoid getting lost in what comes to be framed as "childishness" or "immaturity." They do so to remain close to, to seek safety among, or to vie with others. Concession to these conditions forms the consensus among adults that the shared experiences they undergo form the "real world," while all else failing to conform belongs to the labyrinth.

Their terrified eyes meet me. "Your sister has run off."
I remain silent a moment, then ask, "Do I have a sister?"
My brother Mahmoud responds as though reminding me of something I often forget. "Yeah, yeah, your sister."
"What do you mean my sister?"
He goes on reminding me. "Your sister from your father's other wife."
I look at my father. "His other wife?"
Mahmoud responds, "Yeah, yeah, your sister's run off."

I fall into silence with them, trying to remember. Then my father interrupts my train of thought. "You're the only one of us she

liked. Try to talk with her and see where she is."
"Me?"
Mahmoud: "Yeah, Amr. Try to call her, right away."
I look into Mahmoud's eyes, struggling to comprehend as I say, "Sure, sure, I'll call her."

I go out to the street. It looks like a street in the Arab market quarter of Khartoum, and reminds me of a certain street in Italy, which I've never been to. In the branching side streets young men in gas masks are running from clouds of tear gas. In the distance, the gas clouds fade into a thick fog that rarely covers Cairo.

I sit on a curb shaded by the arcades of a classic-style building, take out my phone, and make a call.
"Yes, who is it?"
"Amr."
"Amr who?"
"Amr your brother."
She yelps and rattles on that everything must

change, that she won't go back, that she won't talk to any of them.

My vision gets lost in the fog, and my hearing gets lost in her furious, clamorous voice. She says a lot, and I lose her train of speech. Then she abruptly calms down and asks me, "What do you think?"
My response: "I'm with you, of course. Take care of yourself and call me if you need anything. I'll tell them you didn't answer my call."
She bursts into tears and says she'd expected that, that I was the only one who would support her. Her tears turn to laughter and she says that she's somewhat reassured now, that she'd been scared to death since she'd left the house.
I smile and say nothing, and she says nothing either for a few moments, catching her breath amidst tears and laughter.
I find nothing to say, so I ask her, "What's your name?"
"Dina," she replies.
"Well, Dina, take care of yourself, and check in to let me know that you're alright. Bye."

I hear her say "bye" in a soft voice, as though she's about to fall asleep.

Heavy exhaustion suddenly overcomes me. I rest my back against one of the arcade's columns shading the pavement, stretch my legs before me, and close my eyes. A group of young men run past, coughing fiercely. My telephone rings and it shows my father's name. I decide I am exhausted enough. I'll turn my phone off and go home and lie to them tomorrow.

There exists no absolute consensus among humans, even among adults, as to what constitutes the "world of reality." Apart from the deep division as to whether God exists, it was remembering dreams that created a massive rift between philosophers, in what was known as the "dream argument." Some philosophers held that dreams, and the images and sounds we remember sensing within them, are evidence that sensual cognizance of images and sounds does not necessarily prove the real existence of what we see and hear. This debate ended with the division of philosophers over the "true" existence of the material world, our recollection of events in the "labyrinth" overriding our conviction of alleged events in "reality."

Rene Descartes, for example, drew upon the dream argument in his methodological skepticism of everything, despite the fact that he turned to philosophy to begin with due to three dreams he had in one night. In the first dream, strong winds pushed him toward a church (classical theology); in the second he found a Latin dictionary and upon opening it, the first phrase he randomly read was "what path in life should I choose?" (philosophy); in the third he found a volume of poetry with a Latin verse reading "what is and what is not" (doubt).

Descartes gave himself over to doubt, distancing himself from classical theology, and yet philosophy ultimately brought him back to God. As a believing philosopher, Descartes called upon God in an attempt to solve the philosophical division over the existence of reality as perceived by our sensual cognizance. He argued there is not sufficient rational proof that our senses imply the true existence of what we sense. Rather, what we believe exists—following a process of doubt, examination, and study—does in fact exist, God willing. And why? Because the guarantor is God, for it was unreasonable in Descartes's opinion for God to have created us and our thoughts of a world that has no existence. Such an illusion does not befit the perfection of God; God would not create an entire world of labyrinths.

Our "philosophy of religion" professor at Cairo University scornfully laid out the gaps in Descartes's thought. He mocked the believing Christian who turned to philosophy after seeing three "night visions" like those of saints, and who then played with philosophical language to support his pre-held faith that he was not bold enough to seriously criticize. At the end of the lecture the professor asserted, his eyes bulging with conviction and his smile wide with confidence, that Islam is the true religion that corresponds to sound philosophy, and that this would be the topic of the following lecture.

In a barber shop I entered for the first time, Slavoj Žižek was the barber. Without my permission, he quickly began trimming my beard. It was too late to object, so I waited until he had completely shaved it off and then angrily got up, saying that I had wanted to cut the hair on my head and not my beard, that I don't shave my beard. He impatiently apologized, frantically fiddling with his shirt and grey beard. I angrily left and he followed me, demanding pay for the shave. I refused, and he pulled out the razor blade and threatened me with it. I ran and he ran after me. Then he stopped abruptly and screamed, "Wait!" So I stopped. He ran back and aggressively pulled down the barber's metal shop front. I waited until he had locked up the shop, and then he ran back to me screaming in accented English, "Welcome to the desert of the real!"

When we try to remember, we usually try to remember "reality," or the "path," but what do we remember of a labyrinth?

I still remember well that intersection where my mother disappeared, leaving me to get lost. I even remember the color of the houses that had changed. I remember how I quickly memorized the way to my grandmother's house through twisting alleys, and how I would traverse the path there and back, solemn and wary.

As companionship
As though God were with us

I was in Alexandria, before the door to a mosque near the sea, the sun over my head. The door was closed so I knocked, and was greeted by Abul Abbas Al-Mursi, who led me inside with a smile. He introduced me to a man sitting before the prayer niche, one of Al-Mursi's pupils in Sufism: Ibn Ata'illah Al-Skandari.

Ibn Ata'illah appeared like a teacher; he was surrounded by who I thought were students. I passed by them to sit directly before him. He asked, "Do you desire to follow the path? Do you accept to be to your sheikh as a corpse in the hands of the person ritually washing it?" In an attempt to joke I replied, "But I am still alive."

With angry and impatient severity he retorted, "People are asleep as long as they are alive, when they die they wake up."

He gestured with his hand to his pupils, and one of them tapped on my shoulder to get up with him, and I did. They all got up and dispersed. The one who had tapped on my shoulder walked with me two steps, and then left me and headed to a corner. Abul Abbas Al-Mursi disappeared, and I left the mosque on my own. I stood outside in the dark night lit only by a faint crescent moon, waiting for a taxi to take me to the Sidi Gaber train station.

I purchased Ibn Ata'illah Al-Skandari's book *Al-Hikam (Wisdoms)* by mistake. I was lost and confused amongst the intertwining paths of religiosity and the paths of the Al-Dokki area around my highschool. Near Al-Dokki square I stopped at a newspaper and book stand. I thought the book's title was *Al-Hukm (Government)*, and on the cover I read that the author was Ibn Ata'illah, an Egyptian Sufi. I had strayed far in Islamic political literature, and the dream of reinstating the caliphate kept me awake at night even as it grew further and further from reality. I hadn't heard of this book and deemed it a discovery. What would Al-Skandari the Sufi have to say about politics and government? Naturally he didn't say anything.

I roamed with the spiritual Wisdoms of Ibn Ata'illah, which took me from my dreams of the world to dreams of obliteration of the world in order to witness the pre-existent, eternal, infinite being. His book remained with me the rest of the day, on the schoolbus, in the last seat in class, at the Orman Gardens to which the schoolboys and girls snuck off together, and in bed.

When he wrote, "God was, and there was nothing with Him; He is now as He was," it did not seem as eloquent to me as my favorite spiritual saying, "Grieve not, for God is with us." Moreover, the only thing I was certain of was that I existed, and if God existed, I'd like Him to be with me, or for me to be with Him. If Ibn Ata'illah did not think that he truly existed, or that he had died and therefore gained consciousness, that was his business. At the end of the day, he no longer existed and I did, and I was fully cognizant and not willing for him to make me dead like he was. When Ibn Ata'illah visited me in a dream, or I visited him, it was as though we knew what each others' souls held, but it didn't seem there would be harmony between us.

I approached the sheikh with a strong physique, piercing eyes, and harsh features. I thought he was Ibn Taymiyyah. I told him what had happened with Ibn Ata'illah Al-Skandari, and he said, "Don't grieve, those who walk with no guide along the path of suppositions and heretic tendencies do not know exactly which path they are taking. If a questioning skeptic follows them, they'll get confused every step of the way. Debate will persist at every crossroad, and they'll split up on more paths than actually meet them, until each is on his own path." Then he leant closer to me and said in colloquial Arabic, "I mean, don't let them bother you. They don't know the path to start with and they're confused enough as it is!" He laughed heartily as he slapped palms with me. He took out two cigarettes and gave me one as we walked through the courtyard of the citadel prison, both of us wearing prisoner uniforms.

Ibn Ata'illah Al-Skandari was a witness in the trial of Ibn Taymiyyah for his thought and for his extreme opinions on Sufism and its leading saints, which were endangering Sufi prestige and influence. A movement was gathering against Ibn Taymiyyah, who had come from Damascus, and together with scholars from the four schools of Islamic law, Sufis filed complaints against him and called for his trial. Ibn Ata'illah filed accusations against Ibn Taymiyyah and incited the judges against him.

It is said Ibn Taymiyyah proudly declared that Ibn Ata'illah was not wrong, and had only spoken the truth of him. When the judges gave Ibn Taymiyyah the option of imprisonment or banishment from Egypt back to Damascus, he chose prison, perhaps because he had also been imprisoned for his thoughts there. In either case, his disciples followed him to prison, visiting him and learning from him, as I did. He told us, "Whatever my enemies do to me, my paradise is in my heart. My imprisonment is a retreat, my murder is martyrdom, and my banishment from my country is a journey."

I told him, "Grieve not, for God is with us." The companionship he held in prison, in his paradise, in his banishment, was more compelling and present than the obliteration, union, and wandering of the Sufis. Together Ibn Taymiyyah, me, and God met the world head-on.

Ibn Taymiyyah was seeking a clear path. I knew him as high-strung, stern-natured, sharp-minded, and stubborn. It was as though he wanted to wake the world from its dreams and have it stick closely to a specific path, one realistic and carefully drawn. He held that scattered dreams threatened the reality of the one path.

In contrast, Ibn Ata'illah, as the rest of the Sufis, was like one who had awakened from reality to find himself in a prolonged intoxication. He was content to remain living a long and delectable dream, one in which he immersed himself after extracting himself from rationality and even existence. He submitted himself to that which he did not fully comprehend, and naturally he relaxed in his confrontation with the world, as the world did in its confrontation with him, such that he sometimes incited my envy, and sometimes my scorn.

The intoxication of Sufis and their contiguous, protracted dreams allow time for loitering in their boundless spaces that can expand or contract, and where everything is open to interpretation. In contrast, Ibn Taymiyyah's path was clear in alerting me that I was leaving it in favor of dreams. And when I did so, my respect remained for the companionship of Ibn Taymiyyah, who, upon announcement of a clear, fair, and compassionate disagreement, bid me farewell at his prison door.

We were no longer together, and God was no longer with us. Perhaps Ibn Ata'illah truly didn't exist, and therefore God wasn't with him either. Perhaps God was in fact alone, and we too were alone, and all of us are now as we were.

I'm on the minbar giving the Friday noon sermon at the mosque of Sultan Hassan. The mosque's imam is standing before me, directly before the minbar, with all the worshippers standing behind him.

I give a very short and enigmatic sermon with

no clear topic. I quote excerpts from Sartre, Woody Allen, and the Damma folkloric songs of Port Said, and tell some jokes. Everyone has a good time and laughs.

Following a spirited joke they like, and for which they applaud, I feel it's an appropriate moment to conclude the sermon. So I sit down and pull out my cell phone and scroll through Facebook and Twitter, following the astonishment over news and video clips of my historic sermon that quickly leaked out.
The Imam climbs two steps of the minbar and says to me, "There's still the second part of the sermon."

I tell him I've finished, and he says, "No way. You have to go on a bit longer before we hold the prayer."

I get up and improvise a serious speech about the importance of hatred in political and social life. I say there lies grave danger in the fact that all presidents, politicians, and sheikhs speak about love while ignoring hatred as an important element in our lives. They must acknowledge that there are segments of the populace who hate the head of government, and that he hates them. There are other segments who hate the sheikhs, and they hate them. We must acknowledge hatred and think about it, and we must manage it wisely. We must create an open outlet for hatred among us; we must liberate our hatred from hidden grudges. We must practice our animosity with courage and morals, and without meanness. I notice the imam has climbed a few steps of the minbar and is elbowing my shin to make me stop talking.

In fact I stop talking, and he rushes to the microphone and voices the call to prayer. Then he says, "We apologize for this sermon as its content changed due to a technical error in the sound system, resulting in content counter to the directives of the Ministry of Religious Endowments and the illustrious Al-Azhar." I climb down from the minbar and pass through the lines of worshippers, who shake my hands in admiration and glee, and remind me of the jokes I'd told. I exit the mosque as the prayer begins.

As prophecy
I see myself slaughtering you

I am largely convinced that Descartes was lying when he told of his three dreams. They appear to me, after the fact, contrived, fabricated to accord with subsequent decisions made in his life and philosophy. Perhaps it has to do with the touch of "faith" guiding his philosophy and methodology, despite its fame as a philosophy of doubt. Or perhaps it's because I don't like Descartes in general.

My friend Karim Ennara accuses me of the like. He says the dreams I write down appear composed, their details insinuating a plot or idea. He questions how I remember all these dreams in the first place. I don't know how to respond; perhaps there is no possible response. Perhaps he doesn't like me enough to believe my dreams.

Dreamers are the only witnesses to their own dreams. When they tell their dreams, they present them as testimony of something that has happened to them, something they saw. A dreamer is the sole witness to a certain incident, one that is removed from any other context, cut off from logic and the nature of things. No one can criticize it, or refute it based on experience or custom or the facts of nature and society. Nor can one claim it is contradictory or inappropriate. The only standard by which we can believe or refute a dream is our faith in its sole witness, or our fondness for them that makes us take them as sincere and credible.

On Emadeddin Street stood the massive awning of the People's Convention. Inside people sat and ate at a long table. At the far end was another, grandiose tent. Guards forcefully took me into it. Mohamed Hassanein Heikal was sitting alone in the center, wearing the distinctive garb of Muammar Gaddafi. Scowling, he asked if I had dreamt of Anwar Al-Sadat, and what the dream's details had been. What had he said to me, and what had I said to him? Glowering all the more, he asked reprehensibly, "Why was Gamal Abdel Nasser not in the dream?"

Was the poet Mahmoud Darwish excused or justified when he said to/of Gamal Abdel Nasser:

"You are not a prophet / but your shadow is green / we live with you / we walk with you / we go hungry with you / and when you die / we try not to die with you."

Great dreamers divide the world into believers and non-believers of their dreams; only such extreme positions can be held on great dreams. Believers of the dream walk, and go hungry, and try not to die with the death of the dreamer. Some choose death so that the dream does not die, so that it is not killed by the non-believers. With this aim, some or many non-believers may die.

Giving credence to dreams and dreamers sometimes involves extreme violence. Dreams provoke struggles and wars as they are transplanted from an incident concerning only its dreamer to incidents of the real world, of a reality we not merely perceive, but rather which we create within or from the world.

Did Ismail (or was it Isaac?) really say, "Father, do as you are commanded," when his father told him, "My son, I saw myself in my sleep slaughtering you." It was the prophetic dream that

Ibrahim saw as essential to make true, an act in the real world with consequences and witnesses.

In this case deeming something as true was not merely an intellectual exercise or a decision made out of sympathy or love. It was a promise to act toward changing the world so as to fall into conformity with a dream.

In the 1950s, some of Gamal Abdel Nasser's political prisoners, and particularly the communists among them, found themselves in a conundrum: they believed in Gamal Abdel Nasser and they believed that his dream—which no one witnessed but him—was also theirs. They considered him a guardian of their dream, or they wished that was the case. From prison they wrote statements validating and supporting him, but Gamal Abdel Nasser wanted to be a prophet and not merely a green shadow, nor even a red one. And there was no avoiding sacrifices.

At a boisterous party in someone's house, Naeem and I entered an empty room to continue our conversation. We found an old desk there, and Naeem placed his glass on it and began inspecting the contents of its drawers. It appears he found something, as he began flipping through papers. He opened the rest of the drawers and rummaged through their contents. He looked at me, and laughing hysterically, said, "This is the desk of Gamal Abdel Nasser."

I suggested we plan to speedily move its contents, but he told me with decisiveness that left no room for discussion that we must take the entire desk, with all its contents, and get out to the street immediately. We took the desk and staggered down the stairs with it and placed it on the sidewalk outside, on a clamorous street in the popular quarter of Imbaba. Naeem took a bottle of wine and two glasses from one of the drawers; he poured and invited me to drink. I alerted him to the fact that we were in the street, in Imbaba. He ignored me in his intoxication. He took his glass and hopped onto the desk, declaring loudly, "By God, by God, I'll turn it into a fried liver cart!"

Yet life cannot always bear such severity, that is the severity of believing or not believing dreams. Even prophecy cannot bear it. With the exception of moments in which dreams clash with reality, or following moments in which dreams conquer and occupy reality, the norm is for the fierceness of grand dreams to be diluted through interpretation, and to dissolve into the flow of reality.

Ibn Arabi interprets the Qur'an's account of Ibrahim's incident differently from others. God's words to Ibrahim, "you have fulfilled the dream" did not imply praise of the prophet for having believed what came to him in his sleep and trying to make the dream a reality, but rather was a rebuke for having believed the symbolism of the dream as reality, forgetting that "dreaming is the attendance of the imagination," as Ibn Arabi says. Ibrahim believed that he was ordered to slaughter his son, whereas God's intention was something other than, or further than, belief of the vision: its interpretation. And thus God redeemed the son with a sacrificial ram.

Whether the ram descended from the heavens or was roaming free on earth, whether God wanted this or the father did, in the end it was interpretation that redeemed both the dream and belief of it. Interpretation saved the life of the son and the prophethood of the father. It rescued reality from the fierceness of imagination.

Radicalism believes in the dreams of slaughter and pays no heed to reality; moderateness redeems reality with the interpretation of dreams.

We began our meeting in a secret location. We were members of a campaign calling for the instatement of the first elected parliament in a Gulf kingdom. We were all from outside the kingdom.

The campaign was a success, elections were held, and the parliament was instated. But we members of the campaign were in a grave crisis. A female member of the campaign, a TV host, was charged with killing the head of the kingdom's Council of Senior Scholars. She had done so in self-defense after he had attempted to "deter her from the reprehensible" as she prepared to broadcast news of the instatement of the first elected parliament.

The members of the new parliament disowned us. They said that circumstances did not allow them to begin their difficult course of action against the king with defense of a woman who had killed a religious scholar.

I admitted to the campaign members that I had also killed a sheikh in the Council of Senior Scholars, and had buried him in the desert. All the members of the campaign began admitting that they had at one time killed one or more members of the Council of Supreme Scholars.

Perhaps this is the reason Sufism became linked with moderateness: Sufis' interest in the interpretation of dreams and the passage through them to a distant and elevated world. Sufism takes dreams far from here, or buries them within, within the self, or within hermitages or deserts, around the gravestones of new prophets. It does so without battles dividing the world, instead announcing an embracement of the world and its people and animals and everything. In Sufis' dreams, imagination does not agitate the world, but rather removes agitation and brings good tidings.

The religious disposition is generally wary of the agitation that dreams can cause, and attempt to protect believers from their influence. Yet dreams cannot be avoided as a factor of prophecy. The Prophet Muhammad said that a true vision is one of fifty parts of prophecy. And thus a part of prophecy is attainable to dreamers. Believers of prophecy are promised a share of dreams, a splitting and sharing that is not meant in the absolute, but rather on condition.

As all powers are with their subjects, the dreams that prophecy shares with its believers must be subordinate dreams. The Prophet Muhammad said that people have three kinds of dreams: glad tidings from God, and these alone are true visions; sorrow and fear, and the source of these is the Devil; and the soul speaking to itself. In another saying he warned: he who the Devil plays with in his sleep should not speak of it.

Glad tidings alone are true, or wished to be true by prophecies and by promises of meaning and reality. In the counsel of prophets and in billboard advertisements: "Dream—Believe your dream—Follow your dream—Fulfill your dream." All on condition that the dream bear glad tidings of meaning and reality, be it God or the nation or pleasure or power or wealth or love (or revolution?). This requires, foremost, belief in the source of the glad tidings, and to willingly receive them. It requires that you persist in your faith despite any counter-temptations from Satan or enemies or pain or weakness or poverty or shortcoming or might (or revolution?)

Would it be possible for us to see a billboard featuring a man about to slaughter his son under the brightly colored slogan: "Follow your dream"?

As a walk
A journey to the marble desert

Over several summer vacations I became utterly preoccupied with walking. Rather than remaining persistent in seeking the way, or in finding companionship, bouts of walking were to me like intermissions, and then turned into a hobby and an autonomous desire. I would wake up eager to go out and walk with no aim.

A childhood friend joined me, at first laughing at the idea and then loving it. We'd begin walking following the noon or afternoon prayer, randomly selecting a direction within or around Imbaba. We'd walk for hours, never stopping to rest at a café or entering a restaurant, yet trying out most of the juice shops. Sometimes we'd have sandwiches, while standing on the street or walking, and we'd enter different mosques and rest for a few minutes after prayer. We'd walk down side streets, and stop for a cold drink at a kiosk and gaze up at the balconies. We combed both sides of the Nile from Imbaba to Maadi, crossing all the bridges over the Nile in both directions. Before we grew completely exhausted, we'd think up a return plan, which could either be walking or seeking the nearest public transportation.

Upon our return we'd have reaped a collection of scenes of characters, streets, and shops we knew nothing about, a compilation of unconnected images and a great deal of chatter, commentary, serious conversation, and joking pratter that would run on for days. I don't recall anything of our conversations those days other than that at the time I had read that Aristotle and his students were called the Peripatetics because they studied thought together as they walked and wandered about. I told my friend that we had surely walked more than they had, and he replied that it would be boring to walk with a teacher or philosopher who spoke to us about the meaning and import of things.

At times our walking turned into an all-consuming activity, to the point that it drove our fathers to grumble, chastising us for becoming loiterers with no aim. At that point I told my friend we needed Aristotle to walk with us in order to grant our walking meaning and avoid our fathers' anger.

Soon afterwards, meaning caught us unaware. It was while we were walking in a narrow side street of Imbaba, gazing at the houses and people. I noticed a large poster of the pop singer Amr

Diab on one of the balconies. It looked like a poster for a new album, but its title was not clear from that distance. As we stared at the poster, trying to work out the album title, a girl appeared beside it. She was my classmate from school.

After summer vacation, at the start of the school year, I had to justify my presence in her narrow street and my staring up at her balcony. Walking aimlessly and then stopping to look at a poster of Amr Diab was not convincing when she asked. I fretted she'd be angry and tell her family, who would tell mine, and then my family would think that this was the meaning behind my daily loitering. Yet she kept this notion to herself, ignoring my response and smiling with childish coquetry and falling silent. I smiled, comfortable with her comfort. She smiled at her imagined meaning to my walk, which was nice in any case. I smiled at the misunderstanding.

She was a nice girl, and our exchanged smiles remained nice. And for some time I would think of her every time I heard Amr Diab sing his song "They blame me": *"Rejoice, my heart / dream, my heart / and walk the path of love to its end."*

The poster had been for the album "They blame me," but of course I avoided passing down her street again.

We were walking within the areas cordoned off around work sites, massive reconstruction taking place in the streets surrounding the Supreme Court. People joined our march in silence as we calmly traversed the streets of downtown engulfed in reconstruction. After walking at length in silence, we reached an open horizon. One of us called out, "We've arrived at Jerusalem!" Another said, "This is where the Al-Aqsa Mosque was."

We stood a few moments in bafflement before an expanse of marble that stretched emptily into the horizon, a marble desert. They said that the entire city had been razed, and that this marble floor had taken the place of everything.

Suddenly we were all wearing the same outfit: jeans and a white t-shirt. The marble expanse filled with people of all nationalities and ethnicities. At its extremities young men distributed juice boxes and bags of crunchy snacks. It was as though it were an opening party, or a closing party, and everyone was happy and excited. Everyone was eating and drinking. Some were lying down on the marble. Some of us were dancing the Palestinian dabke, and others were dancing to inaudible disco. There was a deep silence. No sound other than distant mumblings and the soft whistle of wind sweeping over the marble.

I lay down on the ground, and the nice girl sat down beside me. She said that the ground was warm despite it being otherwise, and she rested her head on my thigh and slept.

Slipping toward meaning is inevitable. People refuse to remember their dreams, as though they were merely aimless walks in a labyrinth with imaginary company, unconnected scenes of people and things and events. They wish dreams were a path to somewhere, glad tidings or a warning or counsel, a sneak preview of the future or a re-enactment of the past. No matter how simple and aimless the walk, people want to view it as a journey that is bewildering and yet holds meaning, if only we could find our way to it.

Based on the phrase used in the Qur'anic verse "If you can interpret [pass through] dreams," Ibn Arabi held that the interpretation of visions and dreams is like a "passage" to their abstracted meanings in the world of the soul and the truth. These meanings, on their way to us, fall into the "attendance of the imagination," assuming material, sensual forms and becoming things, people, and events that sleepers witness, comprehending them with their senses. In the opposite journey to move beyond imagination, interpretation is used to pass over the forms in order to reach their meaning. To Ibn Arabi, imagination in dreams is the bridge, or the path, that meaning crosses, or which we cross back if we are scholars or visionaries like Ibn Arabi.

With Freud, the interpretation of dreams is also a journey in the attendance of imagination, a journey of imagining the primordial form of the world, the images of things disconnected from their usual and familiar associations, their formulation pliable. Downtown Cairo leads to Jerusalem, the features of Jerusalem disappear, the city in its entirety is transformed into an expanse of marble. My experience walking is distinguished from the paths I have walked, and takes me to a Jerusalem of marble.

Freud also aspired to arrive at meaning through the interpretation of such formulations. Yet in his case meaning is not the real world as opposed to, and superior to, the material world, but rather the unconscious (alluded to by the symbolism of the suppressed and the repressed) that the material world beset, stalking it until it fled inwards.

While the conscious engages strategically with the world, or at least tries to, the suppressed unconscious, ever on the flee, only comes out to walk a bit when the conscious is absent.

I was returning from the market with groceries, walking familiar paths near my house. I met neighbors and shopkeepers I know well, but of our house there was no trace. The very idea of it grew hazy in my mind. I no longer held a clear image of it, of the building structure, of where exactly it lay amidst all the familiar details that made me feel I was nearby while the house itself failed to exist.

I came and went, to and fro, with a muddled mind. I'd approach what made me feel I was nearby, and then I wouldn't know which way to turn. My heart beat rapidly, the familiar scenes escalating my fear, and the neighbors' glances unbearable. I rushed away from everything that reminded me of the house, and once I was sufficiently distant, I sat on the ground and tried to catch my breath, although the feeling remained unbearable.

Muhammad gave me a print of the Dome of the Rock in Jerusalem, framed in gold with the Qur'anic verse, "And that they may enter the mosque as they did the first time." Muhammad had been entrusted by the Muslim Brotherhood to befriend me. They were worried about the young man in the School of Engineering who had gone to them of his own accord rather than them approaching him. Moreover this young man's religious tendencies seemed to be fundamentalist at times and philosophical at others, and yet it seemed he had read most of the Muslim Brotherhood's literature. Muhammad's role was foremost to ensure I was not a government informant, and secondly to observe my intellectual formation so they would know how to deal with this strange and enthusiastic young man.

My uneasy position with the Muslim Brotherhood in the School of Engineering did not improve, due to my "confused and distracted intellectual formation," as they put it. Yet despite this they felt safe with me, and engaged me to edit their magazine, at first in the School of Engineering and then for Cairo University at large.

Once Muhammad felt safe with me, he confessed his role and gave me the print. I accepted it, telling him that of course I had sensed his role but was not upset in any way because I liked him. At the time I appreciated his devotion to the

Muslim Brotherhood, even if he had not been truly interested in my friendship, and I hung the print up in my room.

The print intruded on my temperament, which was abstract thanks to fundamentalism and philosophy. I preferred walls that were blank, and ideas that were free from the ornamentation and light preaching that filled Muslim Brotherhood activist rhetoric, and which was typically naïve and superficial.

I had no special feelings towards Jerusalem or even the Kaaba. I did not like such material mediations clad in religious sanctity and either bound to the emotional beings of believers or summoned in order to tie religiosity to political activity: the liberation of Jerusalem begins in Cairo.

I discussed this with Mohamed one day while we worked on engineering sketches in my room. Given that our friendship had now grown strong, I expressed my feelings towards the Dome of the Rock print he had given me, and which now hung over our heads. I told him of my feelings toward the print, and how they related to what I'd like to write in criticism of the Muslim Brotherhood's religio-political rhetoric. Without even raising his eyes from the sketch he was working on, Muhammad said, "You're going to be secular, Amr."

I would have liked to have remembered him as insightful, but he immediately continued, "And it would be best if you finished your sketch instead of philosophizing. You're an engineer, not a philosopher or writer, and you won't ever be, so chill."

When I laughingly reminded him that he was speaking to the editor-in-chief of the Islamic current's university magazine, his insight returned to him as he said, "They'll be firing you soon, trust me. Your thought's distracted and your actions clearly reflect that."

The Muslim Brotherhood withheld the first issue I edited, and it was never printed. They told me I had put together a magazine that more closely resembled the publications of the left than those of the Islamists. I thanked them, and turned to the left.

I lost my passport in Tel Aviv. I was looking for the Egyptian embassy there; I had the address written down in Arabic and Hebrew, but all the street signs were in Chinese. I finally found the embassy, but its guard told me that Egypt had recalled its ambassador that morning and shut down the embassy, and he was the only one left. He allowed me to enter and use the phone, and I called the Ministry of Foreign Affairs in Cairo. I explained in elaborate detail that I was there on a journalistic assignment with permission from the Ministry of Foreign Affairs, but had lost my passport and then found the embassy closed. I asked how I could get back.

The man heard my story to the end without saying a word. He remained silent a moment, and then calmly asked, "You mean you're calling from Israel?"

I impatiently replied that this whole long story meant I was in fact there, and I wanted to return.

Following another moment of silence he replied, "There's no such thing as Israel. Don't call from there again," and hung up.

As enchantment
A meeting with nonexistence

When I asked what she wanted now in order to be happy, she said she wanted to not exist.

As someone who loved her existence, this pained me. I tried to pass over it lightly, and told her I was asking about something I could do.

She smiled and said it was too late now to wish she had never been, but that she could wish to die, and, if sincere, I could make that happen.

This was terrifying.

As her features retracted in sorrow I sometimes felt she was disappearing, or on the verge of death. This scared me, and drove me to make up stories and jokes, simply to see a smile flash across her face, bringing her back to her beautiful existence. I wanted to fix that smile in place. I returned to my studio, trying again and again to draw her. I dreamt of her more than once, although I don't remember more of the dream than the distancing of her dimples and the narrowing of her eyes, and their shine. It was as though I wanted to extract that smile alone from its crisis-ridden existence. I decided to do something, and told her I had an idea that would free her of the existence she wanted rid of. She looked at me in surprise, with curiosity, but without fear. This was also terrifying.

The plane moved on from Khartoum airport. It didn't fly, but rather moved over the ground. It left the airport and moved through the streets. It stopped at traffic lights and crossed bridges and went through tunnels. Then it stopped, and the hostess came to me and asked if I was the one who wanted to go to Cairo. She said we were very close, and that I could get off the plane now before it moves on. I got off, and found my bags scattered in an expansive desert. The plane moved off through the distant sands.

She was there, sitting in an open convertible. She got out and waited for me as I approached. "Why are you so late?," she asked.

She was calm, and didn't act as though I had been away for a month, yet her smile was there. I approached her, and she didn't kiss or hug me; she didn't even shake my hand, but rather we sufficed with exchanging smiles. She asked me where I would put all my bags, then turned to the trunk of the car, searching for something as though it were the first time she'd seen it. She completed her search quickly. Defeated and flustered, she said there was no room for the bags. Her features began to fade. I, too, grew flustered, but quickly replied that the bags were of no relation to me. In a childish manner her smile returned. We got into the car, and as she turned it on she asked if I knew the way from there to Imbaba.

Jean-Paul Sartre held that the relation between consciousness and dreams is one of enchantment, in which we don't sense the anxiety of existence given the open possibilities and freedom of experimentation. Dreams dispossess us of our free being, at times making of ourselves subjects who we watch. Our freedom to choose within a dream seems somehow removed from us; we act and we watch ourselves act. Perhaps we get scared or confused, but these are all spontaneous manifestations that lack the existential anxiety accompanying life decisions and their conflicts with the past or future. In dreams, we are creatures liberated from their crisis-ridden existences. Even the crises in dreams fail to provoke a sense of responsibility within us. Cruel and harsh things may happen to us and we remain subjects lacking independent will or gods with free will and a clear conscience.

Enchantment always wrests away a certain degree of will, as is the case with love. We are enchanted by our desire if we are unable to resist it. If it overwhelms our will, there is no way out from captivity except through the misery and pain that comes with crossing the breach we must carve in our souls between will and desire. Either that, or we must love our captivity and surrender to it completely. We must be pleased that our will and desire are in harmony, that our freedom is extinguished before love, that we are comfortable within enchantment as though in a dream.

As she left her workplace for the last time after resigning, she raised her hands high and screamed. She had left her family home and moved in with me, which required that we marry and so we quickly did, without preparations or negotiations with family. The only negotiations held were that we had decided not to enter into negotiations with them regarding our life. Now she felt existence stretching out before her, after the suffocation of life in her family home had driven her to work she hated just to be out of the house, and the suffocation of life at work she hated had driven her to stay in the family home she hated. Now we were fully immersed in enchantment with our absolute freedom, our victory over her crisis-ridden existence. Yet was this an ultimate victory? Can enchantment live on in the heart of absolute freedom?

For months she sat like a child turning her free existence about like a difficult and confusing toy. Her sense that she was free and must do something drew close and dispelled the enchantment. Now the anxiety of existence was returning, emerging through the schism between will and desire. She wanted something, but felt no desire for anything. She truly didn't want to exist, and I had no other plan. I snatched away a knife she had pointed at her chest, but I wasn't able to make her smile. She looked at me for a long time without smiling, and her star began to set even as she clung to me.

We were fully engrossed in work. She burst into the room with a confidence appropriate to her svelte stature and stylish look. "How are you all?," she asked in a mirthful, flirtatious tone.

We turned to her. Some of my colleagues were puzzled, but I smiled. It seemed that no one knew her but me. I can't say I actually knew her, but I remembered her. She had been beside me at a boisterous party, at the drinks table, when she'd suddenly said out of context, "I only drink whiskey."

"Try wine," I'd suggested.

"No, I only drink whiskey," she'd repeated.

Her face now looked completely different.

Less attractive. Yet I had no doubt it was her, and not because she was holding a bottle of whiskey.

She raised the bottle and said, "What do you think about having a glass together?"

My colleagues attempted to excuse themselves as being busy with finishing the film. She replied that she could help us with our work. They fell silent, and she welcomed that and encouraged them. With circumspection, they accepted the offer of help from the strange girl.

We all got up and went to a massive sink. She opened her bottle and poured the whiskey out. My colleagues poured other bottles into the sink, and then emptied into it bottles of detergent and bags of fruit. One of them pressed a button and the liquids in the sink slowly mixed, combining their colors and scents.

We waited in a spacious hall entirely painted in black. A group of us went and brought glasses they filled from the sink. We took small sips and mumbled in agreement, "The film is charming, the film is lovely."

She was drinking calmly. She still had the face of another girl.

In Milan Kundera's novel *Identity*, Jean-Marc excitedly travels to his beloved, Chantal. When he arrives at the hotel, he goes to the beach to look for her. In his haste, he nearly gets into an accident that could have cost his life. He catches sight of her from afar, instantly recognizing her familiar frame that to him has always meant happiness. He rushes over, calling out and waving, but she pays no note. When he draws close and sees her face, he finds it one other than Chantal's. It is the face of an old woman, less beautiful than Chantal, looking at him in a manner indicating she does not know who he is. She isn't Chantal; she's another woman.

"Mistaking the physical appearance of the beloved for someone else's," wrote Kundera, "How often that's happened to him! Always with the same astonishment: does that mean that the difference between her and other women is so minute? How is it possible that he cannot distinguish the form of the being he loves the most, the being he considers to be beyond compare?"

Jean-Marc returned to his room and found Chantal there, her face truly less beautiful and her glance hateful. She said that she hadn't slept well, but he felt that the woman he had waved to on the beach had taken her place forever.

Jean-Marc has a dream reflecting that. In his dream, he recognizes Chantal from afar. When he approaches, he is certain it is her; even when he sees another face with her body, he is positive it is her. In his dream, even though her face is different, she is always Chantal. The moment he awakens, he looks for her beside him. He gazes at her face he knows and pronounces her name, as though he wants to summon back her singular identity.

Details can toy with consciousness, misleading it and tricking it. Yet consciousness is insistent in pursuing the truth via the senses, intuition, and logic, with the aim of making its way out of the labyrinth. Dreams go even further; they toy with existence and reality. They deny the "real" in existent things, and reveal their innate "nonexistence," as Sartre says.

Jean-Marc's delusions of Chantal begin to separate from her and then distance themselves. It becomes possible for the image of Chantal to persist even after her existence ends. Jean-Marc's fancies of Chantal can grow in number and variety; there can be more than one Chantal. Imagination can play with her image as though it were the painting of an imaginary figure and the artist could change his mind regarding the form of her frame or the appearance of her face, or even the very principal of her existence, as though it were an imagined presence conjured up out of nothing by the imagination, and which could also be pushed back into nothing.

Chantal is truly an imaginary figure in a novel, and so is Jean-Marc.

I was sitting with her, and we were trying to extend bridges of familiarity based on what we knew of each other through Facebook in order to overcome the awkwardness of a first meeting. Yet she appeared and approached us, she herself, or another copy of her. She came and greeted herself, or her first copy, with warmth, and greeted me with a restrained friendliness appropriate to our old but distant acquaintance via Facebook. She exchanged a few words with herself, and asked her if she and I were friends. She told herself that we were friends on Facebook, but this was the first time we'd met face to face. More precisely: face to two faces. She looked from herself to me, trying to guess whether this was an ordinary meeting or a date. She was so open about it that she embarrassed us. She cut off her guessing and said she'd leave, apologizing for intruding. She took another look to see our response to her apology and whether we'd ask her to sit with us. We didn't, and she raised her hand to bid farewell to me in an appropriately reserved manner, but with a wide, contrived smile. Then she kissed herself goodbye and said she'd see her in a bit and that she had some things to tell her.

As a battle
What we could suffer

In the days when I might have ended my proselytizing posts with #the_revolution_continues, I tried more than once to read Hannah Arendt's *On Revolution*. I kept stopping part way through the introduction, when she mentions that key phrase of a Greek historian about war: "The strong did what they could, and the weak suffered what they must."

I'd stop at this point, thinking about what we could do and what we must suffer. I'd grow preoccupied, thinking aloud with strong/weak companions on Facebook and Twitter, and in posts, videos, articles, seminars, meetings, marches, and demonstrations. I'd lose myself to the companionship of enchantment and forget to go on with the book.

It wasn't long before it became clear what we could do, what they could do, and what we all must suffer. The labyrinth grew all the more complicated, while dreams, in all their varieties, grew increasingly harsh. Beside #the_revolution_continues, I began adding to my posts what Albert Camus attributed to Sisyphus, #with_neither_despair_nor_hope. I did so with a touch of bitterness and a great deal of mirth.

Later still and following much resistance, bitterness gained the upper hand, although mirth did not entirely disappear. I began ending my few posts with just #with_neither_despair_nor_hope.

> *I noticed Hannah Arendt on the Nile Corniche, wearing a modest dress and with her head uncovered, that distinctive garb worn by Christian women in the popular quarters. She was walking with some difficulty, and had just come out from Al-Warraq Church. She was looking for something.*
>
> *She stood for a while until a microbus arrived. She struggled to climb in, leaning on two young men, and sat by the window. As the microbus drove on, she looked at me and raised her hand, gesturing to me with the two-fingered "victory" sign, and smiled.*

When I first got to know the word "revolution," when I was young, I imagined it was an epic moment during which all ordinary life halted. All the people came out the streets, all the shops closed, and all work halted. No shop could remain open during the revolution; no bus or microbus or taxi could traverse the streets during the revolution. All open shops would be stormed, all moving vehicles would be destroyed. People would march, gather in demonstrations, engage in clashes. No one would go anywhere except for the revolution. No one would do anything outside of the revolution. All people, and all moments, would be dedicated to the battle. I couldn't imagine what people would eat or how they'd live. I only imagined how they would die, how they would kill each other, until it ended with an overwhelming victory for one side over the other. The revolution would be named after the victors, and a new life would begin under this victory.

Nietzsche was sitting on a bench outside a villa in Al-Moqattam, wearing a dark traditional Egyptian gown. It was not the first time I'd seen him there. This time I stopped and raised my hand in greeting, thinking about which language I should greet him in. He beat me to it with an Upper Egyptian dialect. Frowning, his lips strongly pushing his thick moustache, he said, "And may peace and God's mercy and blessings be upon you, Pasha. Can I be of service?"

The evening of January 25, once the security forces had dispersed us and we'd been chased from Tahrir Square, we found ourselves in large groups in downtown Cairo, and so kept on demonstrating. When the security forces again broke up the numerous demonstrations near the square, these split into a larger number of smaller demonstrations running from downtown into the surrounding neighborhoods. I felt that the moment had begun to gain significance. This was not just a demonstration that came to an end, this was the Big Moment.

Ultimately I found myself near dawn demonstrating with a group in the Sabtiyya neighborhood. One of us climbed atop an electricity box in the dark street and gave a speech, declaring we wouldn't stop demonstrating until the people woke up and came out to join us, the demonstrations continuing until the fall of the regime.

When I noticed a taxi approaching, I was astonished to see it there amidst the revolution. All other vehicles had been speeding away from the marches in fear, yet this taxi approached us and stopped nearby. Its appearance snapped me out of the ongoing Big Moment. I saw the street's residents awakening to the sound of our chants and the demonstrator s speech, looking sleepily down at us from their balconies, rubbing their eyes, and some of them going back inside unperturbed. I remembered that I could sleep a little. Maybe I could eat something. Perhaps I could go and write something while drinking a glass of wine. Maybe we could meet in cafés after the demonstrations, and celebrate in the evening after the meetings. Perhaps I could grow tired of the revolution and travel for a month to Sudan and spend all my time reading Shakespeare and listening to Sudanese music and completely avoiding any news from Egypt. I could return and become preoccupied for months with a love story. Perhaps I could invite her to dinner, or to a demonstration, or to clashes. Perhaps some of us would die in clashes, and some of us would go to the funeral and others to prison or the beach or abroad or to the enemy lines. Perhaps I could get busy writing a long research paper or my prolific dreams, or with following the news from the newspaper editorial office and the satellite channel studio. Perhaps I could return from the office and studio to break up the pavement and throw stones at the enemy, and then rest to the side and buy some crunchy snacks from a snack vendor on the corner and follow the cat and mouse chase, and the dead and the injured, until the enemy overruns us and I quickly join the defeated and we all run away.

My musician neighbor Mohamed Adel found himself at midnight in a building under construction surrounded by the police. He was rushing to and fro with his guitar; I don't know if he was seeking an escape or a place to hide. I was behind him, filming with a hand-held camera. I knew the police had surrounded the building to arrest a group of people who had attempted to hold a zar spirit placation ritual without a license.

My neighbor found himself face to face with the building's guard. I quickly surmised that the guard was in cohort with the police, and possibly the one to have reported the zar gathering.

I intervened, putting my camera away, and said to the guard, "We're not the people who were doing the zar, we're the spirits they summoned. They held the zar without a license but we want to go in peace, so please help us get out of here or else we'll have to hurt you."

The taxi driver who had approached our gathering by the electricity box said, "Anyone going towards Imbaba?"

I noticed we had begun to decrease in number, and that some of us were debating with the speech-giver the necessity of splitting up now and reconvening tomorrow, and how and where to meet then. I got into the taxi with a few others, and the driver asked what we were doing at that late hour. One of us told him, "The revolution's begun." He said he hadn't heard about any revolution on the radio. My house was the farthest away, and when he got me there at the end of the ride, he laughed and said, "If this revolution of yours doesn't succeed, I know where all of you live, champs."

I crept with the film crew and we hid beside the prison wall. The production assistants blew up part of it, and Alaa Abdel Fattah was waiting for us right on the other side. He quickly exited from the opening made as sirens roared.

I gave my orders to the cameramen and stopped Alaa, asking him to slow down so we could film. He screamed at us, "Are you mad? What the hell are you filming?"

He ran with his family members Manal, Mona, and Sanaa—we had asked them to attend the breakout—as I and the film crew ran alongside. As the crew filmed, I tried to calm Alaa, and to convince him that we had all just committed a major crime. Trying to escape would not serve us well; we would return to prison sooner or later, so it would be best to let us shoot this film, because it was so lovely to shoot this film.

As a blank space
Who draws all this nothingness?

The first message she sent to me after we parted ways was an angry one in which she asked me to stop mentioning her in the dreams I write down. I read the message in anger, and we bickered a little through text messages:
–I don't write your name!
–You mean me by "the nice girl"!
–How could anyone know you're "the nice girl"?
–You know that my boyfriend is crazy about your writing!
–Thanks for the compliment!
–You're welcome, but he knows, and now he's going crazy because of these dreams!
–Why couldn't it be anyone else?
–You write my details well!
–Thanks again for the compliment!
–Thanks for the vulgar dream in which I agree to marry you in return for a bottle of wine!
–It was just a dream!
–I wish these dreams would stop!
–I wish!

And then the dreams truly stopped.

I had been furious when we ended this argument.

I tossed the laptop beside me on the white mattress set upon the white ceramic tiled floor stretching across the living room with white walls and free of any furniture.

Following my argument with "the nice girl," I dreamt of her one last time. Massive, dense tattoos covered her body, and her fingers clung to my neck as I tried to free myself.

I wrote the dream down and removed her epithet as "the nice girl," and thus she failed to recognize herself. After that she disappeared from my dreams entirely. Either that, or I no longer remembered my dreams of her. I was impressed with the will of my dreams, or of my selective memory roaming free within dreams and enchantment. I convinced myself of this and liked the idea. All that remained was to move beyond my lucid memory and buy some furniture.

Until that time, the empty white spaces continued to occupy my dreams, their details condensing within my memory as it distanced itself from the past, occasionally glancing back to observe the distance covered and reminding me to feel my neck.

I avoided the places she frequented for nearly
a year. Then shortly before January 2011, we
had a friendly, yet tense meeting. I had prepared
myself to appear mature and over it all, and
she controlled her words to appear friendly in
a way that promised nothing. In Tahrir Square
we exchanged the typical embraces of friends,
exuberant that we were meeting at the sit-in.
In celebration we went to the movies the day
after Mubarak stepped down, and despite the
excitement of the "revolution's victory," which
provided a poetic background, it was clearly the
beginning to a relaxed friendship that wouldn't
dream of being more.

We were colleagues in political activities and
at work. Once, we argued a great deal and she
made up with me just to ask how I had overcome
my love for her, because she didn't know how to
overcome her feelings for her boyfriend since they
had split up.

She wasn't very nice, as is obvious, yet I replied
with the fidelity of an ex-lover:
—I let go of all defense mechanisms, and didn't tell
myself that my love had been insignificant or my

desire superficial, despite your abuse and horrible behavior!
—Thanks for the compliment!
—I faced the problem and told myself: it was beautiful and I wanted it very much, but it slipped away from me, and when I held onto it, I was humiliated!
—Humiliated?
—Yes, I was humiliated. But no problem my dear, it's not the end of the world, and it won't be the last time.

A few days later she wrote a long post about an experience of desertion and loss and attempts to move on, and at the end she wrote "I was humiliated," with a laughing emoji.

It was nice of her despite the sensitivities, which I now felt were placed before me to contemplate rather than being cloven into my neck. Eventually I barely remembered them.

During the worst moments of our "defeat," she wrote, swearing bitterly, and extending her curses to the revolution:
—Cursing the revolution is a defense mechanism

we use to escape with.
—How can we live with this shit without a defense mechanism?
—In the same way.
—What way?
—By acknowledging that we took part in something grand and beautiful.
—Thanks for the compliment!
—You're welcome, but it slipped out of our hands, and when we tried to hold onto it we were humiliated!
—Only humiliated?
—We were humiliated horribly! And we'll likely keep getting humiliated! But no problem my dear, it probably won't be the end of the world, and I hope it won't be the last time (smiling emoji).

She asked if I had dreamt of her again, and whether at times I thought of her as a lover. I told her I hadn't dreamt of her since she got angry over my penned dreams. I didn't mention the final dream for the sake of keeping to the clear and proper bounds of the story, but also to loosen her fingers that had been clinging to my neck. I thought about ignoring the second part of the question, but after some mutual silence I said, with a lukewarm nod, that perhaps I had thought so, once or twice.

She grew furious and left. She didn't return, and I didn't contact her, and we never spoke again. It was the last time.

> *The line was long but I didn't join. I met Ahmed Naji at the door and greeted him. We quickly entered via another door, then parted ways inside. It was a spacious exhibition hall soaring in white. There were white beds and chairs, old home appliances, manual washers, old-fashioned irons, and old, primitive implements for preparing tea and coffee. There were small, old, black-and-white televisions. On the wall near the door were the exhibition guidelines: take off your clothes; keep only your underwear on; choose a task: washing clothes or ironing or making tea and coffee for those washing; turn on the nearest television and watch it as you are working or waiting; photographers and videographers will pass by you.*

The rest of the exhibition walls bore photos of previous visitors in underwear, washing and ironing and drinking tea and coffee and smoking. On an old black-and-white television were shots of them undertaking these activities, and looking at other photos on the walls of previous visitors doing the same.

As I walked about I met Naji again, standing in a corner smoking and drinking coffee. He was fully dressed and I asked him about that. He said he was one of the organizers of the exhibition, but that he had taken his clothes off and participated previously. He asked why I hadn't taken my clothes off like the rest of the public, and why none of the organizers had come to me and told me that I must follow the directives.

The art teacher came over to me, an astonished smile on her face. She placed her palm on my shoulder and leant over me, pointing to the completely blank white sheet of paper before me. In a whisper she asked why I hadn't started drawing a picture of peasants destroying the railroad tracks to cut off the path of the English occupation forces during the 1919 revolution. The students in the final year of primary school around me were absorbed in drawing. I was talented in art, and I was an exemplary student who had been at the top of the school for years. A bit flustered, I told her I didn't want to draw a picture of peasants destroying the railroad tracks to cut off the path of the English occupation forces during the 1919 revolution.

She laughed and asked me if I had a problem with the 1919 revolution or with Saad Zaghloul. I laughed at her laugh and said nothing. I almost relaxed, but her smile disappeared as she removed her palm from my shoulder and sternly said that this was the subject of today's class and I must draw a picture of peasants destroying the railroad tracks to cut off the path of the English occupation forces during the 1919 revolution.

The art teacher was olive, toned, and svelte; to a large degree she resembled the pop singer and actress Ruby. Her smile, and the sparkle of her eyes as I drew in class for three consecutive years, were the first things that came to mind when people asked me what I'd like to be when I grew up, so I'd say I'd be an artist. Her stern attempts to make me draw a picture of peasants destroying the railroad tracks to cut off the path of the English occupation forces during the 1919 revolution formed a sudden transformation after three years of spoiling, compliments, and praise.

I refused absolutely, and she insisted to know the reason but I didn't have a reason. Having run out of patience, she let me be, giving me until the next class a few days away to submit my picture. A few days later, I opened before me a completely blank white sheet of paper and stubbornly said that I didn't want to draw a picture of peasants destroying the railroad tracks to cut off the path of the English occupation forces during the 1919 revolution. It appears she felt insulted and challenged, but she held in her anger.

She complained about me to the school principal and to my mother, and they all considered this evidence that my being spoiled had ruined me, and that I had started to be negligent and to rebel. Over the next few days they spoke numerous times in an attempt to understand why they wanted me and why I didn't want to draw a picture of peasants destroying the railroad tracks to cut off the path of the English occupation forces during the 1919 revolution.

When my mother, at a loss, told my father about this, he too was puzzled and called for me. He told me that if I still wanted to be an artist, I must practice drawing everything and be prepared to draw anything. I asked, "So I can't be an artist if I draw many other pictures but don't want to draw a picture of peasants destroying the railroad tracks to cut off the path of the English occupation forces during the 1919 revolution?"

He fell silent a moment, then laughed heartily and said, "No, you're right. You'd be a real artist, you son of a dog, damn me and the peasants and the English and the 1919 revolution!"

He turned to my mother and sternly told her that this matter must be closed immediately, and she must inform the school that his father, too, didn't want him to draw a picture of peasants destroying the railroad tracks to cut off the path of the English occupation forces during the 1919 revolution.

Cairo is under steady and fierce shelling. Planes soar at low elevation. The streets gradually grow dim. I am downtown, running aimlessly with the people.

The shelling stops a few minutes, and people calm down a bit. They stop, and look up at the sky in astonishment and fear.

During a lull in the shelling, people begin to exchange theories: Israel, America, Ethiopia, Iran, Qatar and Turkey taking revenge on the Muslim Brotherhood, the army teaching the people a lesson.

The shelling resumes, this time more fiercely. Downtown has become an expanse of ruin, filled with mounds of collapsed and sindering buildings. As far as the eye can see, there are no tall buildings left.

My running takes me to the area around the Egyptian Railway station, which has not been shelled. It occurs to me that leaving Cairo might be a good idea. Inside the station I find crowds around a train. Masses are trying to convince the drivers to take off. One of them is convinced. I jump with the crowds onto the train.

Communications are completely cut off. No telephone lines or internet. The people piled into the train car exchange the same theories. The typical arguments between supporters of the President, supporters of the Muslim Brotherhood, and supporters of the revolution who hate both sides.

We reach Al-Mansura. There is no shelling here, but people have vacated all the buildings in fear and have filled the streets. It's extra crowded around mosques and churches. Crowds of people are torn between wanting to enter and seek shelter in a mosque or church, and fear of being shelled. There are groups near cafés and restaurants, and others scattered on sidewalks and in gardens.

The groups have begun to engage in discussion and debate. Talk going beyond the typical arguments has led to consideration as to what we should do. All television and radio broadcasts have been halted, and people are transmitting news between the gathered groups. A narrative begins to spread among the people: the US president, contacted the President and rebuked him because the government press still speaks of American conspiracies against Egypt. The US president arrogantly said that if America wanted to attack Egypt, it would attack it head on, without any need for conspiracies. The President was infuriated, and they got into an argument and Trump ended the call angrily, and then the American planes took off.

Within hours the shelling had destroyed the presidential palace. There was debate as to whether the President had been killed or had escaped to a safe place. The buildings of the ministries of the interior and foreign affairs, and the Cairo and Giza security directorates, were all destroyed, as well as a large number of army compounds, the

Tahrir bureaucratic headquarters, and all the buildings of downtown Cairo, in addition to City Stars Mall—there was special interest in the destruction of City Stars Mall—and also Al-Azhar and Al-Hussein Mosques. Widely circulated in discussions was the observation that no churches had been harmed.

I walked among the groups of people, and found myself near a small gathering, at the center of which stood men in full suits. One of them was speaking calmly, and people were addressing him as "Doctor." This doctor said, "There are no indications of a foreign occupation, but what will take place following the destruction of Cairo and the collapse of the central state is the dissolution of society. We'll begin forming sociological study groups, as we'll be obliged to build our society anew."

Freud doubts there is a relation between what we think we remember from a dream and what actually happened in it. Truly, what guarantees that what comes to our minds when we awaken is the same as what we saw when we were asleep?

Perhaps consciousness takes rein the moment we awaken and quickly tries to make amends for the slip of consciousness we've undergone. It rapidly creates a story, or reorders the scattered events of the dream in a more cohesive form, even if it retains certain expanses of the strange and bizarre.

Perhaps it is for this reason that Walter Benjamin advises those who want to remember their dreams not to eat breakfast or start their day's activities upon awakening. Rather they should enact a ritual or pray, such activities belonging to the imagination or otherwise confiding in other worlds. This, Benjamin argues, could help in keeping consciousness and the real world at a distance from what has happened during sleep, so that one's dreams could reach the memory untouched.

Yet what if dreams themselves are a memory or a recollection? What if we remember our experiences in our dreams, in a manner seeking liberation from the world and our circumstances? Like a memory liberated from ourselves, hiding and refusing to give in, refusing to join our lucid memory of which we remain in possession. Like a memory that can only function when we grow distant from our lives through sleep, fleeing from us when we return to consciousness and attempt to grab ahold of it.

It might slip away from us entirely. Or it might partly slip away, part of it remaining to whet our appetites. The memory that slips away enchants us, and worries us when it suggests that our lives might be something other than what we know, or what we think we know and what we can remember. This suggests we are not only what we know about ourselves, and not only what we can remember.

Or perhaps dreams are a memory that merely aims to play with what's happened, or who we've been, and who we wish or fear becoming, with what enchants us, astonishes us, and frightens us, what we wait for, and what takes us by surprise. When this memory confronts our consciousness, or we confront it by waking up, it rips apart what it has created, tossing pieces of it here and there. It disappears in a most cunning and absurd manner, while we scramble to gather its snippets of images, sounds, and words. It leaves us to face the never-ending paths via which we may remember our dreams.

I arrived at the airport, and waited in the spacious annexed sports hall. Everything in it was white: the floor, walls, ceiling, and the few scattered benches.

I was there waiting for someone to take me to a conference. I watched as carpenters and painters made things from pieces of wood all painted white. I began noticing small cockroaches swarming beneath us. They were very small, but also very apparent in this white expanse.

A group of men and women in official, stately, white attire and dark sunglasses entered. They were in a rush and extremely tense. One of them asked us, "Is there a poet here?"

I looked at the workers and the workers looked at me. It appeared I was the only stranger there, but no one replied.

*One of the women repeated the question,
"If you please, is there a poet here? If one is
present, tell us, we desperately need a poet."*

*No one responded. The workers went back to
their work, and I continued observing them
and the roaches swarming beneath the feet of
the well-groomed group in official suits.
It seemed to me like an opening of a poem.*

Indexes

Index of noted figures

Alaa Abd El-Fattah (b. 1981)
"The pink dragon," a friend, political activist, and political prisoner over different periods of time. He fostered Egyptian blogging by founding the Egyptian Blog Aggregator. His blogs and his political activism were and remain an inspiration to multitudes wishing for change, as they were and remain a severe provocation to the dull-witted sectors of state and society. As punishment for this, he remains, until publication of this book, in prison.

Gamal Abdel Nasser (1918–1970)
Father of the Egyptian Republic. To this day, Egyptian and Arab political thought is trying to free itself from his dream and his patriarchalism.

Muhammad Adel (b. 1977)
A friend and musician. He's a prominent guitar player, and a former neighbor of mine in the Muqattam neighborhood of Cairo. He hung on his apartment door a sign reading "sadness is important." He has made charming contributions to writings on depression and the harshness of life, all with mirth and acceptance, which shows in how he sometimes identifies himself as a "bohemian artist who does whatever the others like him to do."

Ibn Arabi (1164–1240)
A celebrated Sufi and the first contemporary artist in Islam. In his writings there is no distinction between, on the one hand, his real-life experiences and political and religious thought, and on the other, his dreams and daydreams. He wrote a curious text titled "Epistle of Good Tidings," in which he recorded his "sermonizing dreams," most of which I do not believe. He said he did not mention among them dreams that referred to his greatness or his spiritual standing, and he intimated in some of his writings that he was more important than the prophets. Ibn Taymiyyah referred to him as a godless infidel. His vast contemporary audience, from Sufis to artists to non-Muslims, hates Ibn Taymiyyah and his fans.

Hannah Arendt (1905–1975)
A German-born American philosopher and political theorist. She's visited me in many dreams, perhaps because she's among the few prominent

females among so many other male philosophers. Or perhaps it's because I have not read enough of her work, which I really must do.

Ibn Ata'illah Al-Skandari (1260–1309)
An Egyptian Sufi. He was a foe of Sufism until his position changed under the tutelage of Abul Abbas Al-Mursi, whose tomb in Alexandria is a landmark. The most important of Al-Skandari's writings is his book *Al-Hikam* "The Wisdoms," amongst the most charming of Sufi literature and the most expressive of the trends running counter to existentialism and conceptualizations of human agency. It was this book that made Ibn Ata'illah Al-Skandari more celebrated than Abul Mursi Al-Abbas amongst Sufi circles around the world, with the exception of Alexandria. Al-Skandari died in Cairo and was buried in an obscure tomb at the base of Cairo's Muqattam Heights. I can't forget what's been said of his colluding with Egypt's judges and Islamic jurisprudents on the imprisonment of Ibn Taymiyyah for his vehement criticism of Sufism.

Karim Ennara (b. 1983)
A friend and researcher specialized in security and police policies. Perhaps this is the reason he doubted the credibility of my recorded dreams, not because he doesn't like me.

Sigmund Freud (1856–1939)
His book *The Interpretation of Dreams* is very long and for the most part boring. I found great difficulty in reading it in its entirety, yet read significant sections after encouraged by Amira Adham, a poet and psychologist. During a three-hour phone call she summarized it in a way that made me want to read it, and I thank her for that.

Mohamed Hassanein Heikal (1923–2016)
Egypt's most prominent political journalist due to the close relationship he had to Gamal Abdel Nasser and the ruling circles of the Arab world and beyond. He was an eloquent mouthpiece for the Nasserist era. In the 1990s and 2000s, I was surprised to find myself enjoying his lengthy articles despite the fact that his distance from the circles of decision-making during that period meant he no longer had anything of value to say, and yet he kept trying to make it appear as though he did.

Milan Kundera (b. 1929)
Reading his novels always consoles me. It's the lightness in humans, life, and love that he revels in stripping bare and which weighs down my heart and pains me existentially, lightening the weight of all else that has happened or could happen.

Mohamed Naeem (b. 1977)
A friend, politician, and leftist writer, sometimes hailed as the "general" due to his strategic and tactical observations and his knowledge of the layout of the revolution's battles and their unfortunate losses. I recommend consulting him in forthcoming revolutions. Our first meeting was in the editorial board of the leftist magazine *Al-Busla* (Compass), whose agenda included liberating leftist thought from the chains of its nationalist Nasserist leaning. When I told him my dream of him, he assured me that he would in fact like to turn Gamal Abdel Nasser's desk into a fried liver cart.

Ahmed Naji (b. 1985)
A friend, novelist, storyteller, and journalist. He identifies himself on Twitter as a "writer and criminal." He was sentenced to two years in prison for "violating modesty" in his novel "The Use of Life" after a chapter was published in the literary periodical "Akhbar Al-Adab," but the court of cassation overturned the ruling and ordered a retrial and his release. His defiant imagination reminds me of Ibn Arabi, and his aggressive nature reminds me of Ibn Taymiyyah. For this reason I rarely get angry with him, and he often visits me in my dreams.

Friedrich Nietzsche (1844–1900)
Sometimes I imagine him as the European Ibn Taymiyyah, or Ibn Taymiyyah as the Nietzshe of Islam.

Jean-Paul Sartre (1905–1980)
The philosopher of existentialism, close to my heart. His name is mostly affiliated with depressing things such as existential anxiety and nausea. Yet I prefer what he wrote and lived of enchantment, and commitment to life and dreams.

Ibn Taymiyyah (1263–1328)
A Muslim scholar and the most prominent theorist of the fundamentalist *salafi* school of thought. He was prolific in his refutations of Muslim philosophers, other Islamic schools of thought, and the Sufis, demonstrating their misguidance, godlessness, and the necessity that some be killed. His popular victory over them is still felt today, and forms a serious problem for Muslims and the world at large. His political views were clear, bold, and magnanimous, making all scholars of official and Sufi establishments despise him, whereas the contemporary jihadist movement adores him. No matter what he's done or caused, for personal reasons I simply can't hate him.

Slavoj Žižek (b. 1949)
A Slovenian philosopher, theorist, and cultural critic. He thinks, speaks, and writes with an enthusiasm and vitality that is contagious. His deep-rooted beliefs make him view the continued existence of capitalism as merely a long dream just as imaginary as the dream of communism.

Index of dreams

A

Why was Gamal **Abdel-Nasser** not in the dream? —3
Wine and liver on the desk of Gamal **Abdel-Nasser** —8, 41
Sartre and Woody **Allen** in the Friday Sermon —32
American airforces strike Cairo —103-106
Hannah **Arendt**, *On Revolution*, 1963 —81-82
Contemporary **Art** —98-99

B

Žižek's **barbershop** —19
The form of the most **beloved being** —74-76
Breakfast —107
The Muslim **Brotherhood** —58-61, 103-104

C

American airforces strike **Cairo** —103-106
The liberation of Jerusalem begins in **Cairo**? —58-60
The return of the **Caliphate** —26
Child in the labyrinth —12-13
Street signs in **Chinese** —62
Wind pushing towards **church** —17
Take off your **clothes** and choose a task —98-99
Cockroaches —109
The **communists** and the red shadow —40
Thanks for the **compliment** —93-97
Contemporary art —98-99
As a **corpse** in the hands of the person ritually washing it —25
The killing of the **Council** of Senior Scholars —43-44

D

Defense Mechanisms —95-96
Descartes and God's Plan —17-18, 37
Slavoj Zizek, *Welcome to the **desert** of the real!*, 2002 —19
The schism between will and **desire** —71
#with_neither_**despair**_nor_hope —81-82
Amr **Diab**, "They blame me," 1994 —52-53
The Latin **dictionary** —17
We try not to **die** with you —39

The **disappearance** of the house —58
The **disappearance** of the mother —10, 20
The **Dome** of the Rock —58-60
The **dragon** in the garden —12
The **dream** of the Big Moment —84-85
Follow your **dream** —46
You have fulfilled the **dream** —42
A share of **dreams** —45
If you can pass through **dreams** —56

E
Enchantement —69-71, 81, 94
What can my **enemies** do to me? —29
The School of **Engineering** —50
A picture of peasants destroying the railroad tracks to cut off the path of the **English** occupation forces during the 1919 revolution —100-103
Karim **Ennara** doesn't like me —37
The suppressed **escapes** —57

F
Face to two faces —77
The **film** in the sink —73-74
Fingernails in the neck —94-97
Following directives —99
#Free Alaa —88-89
Free being —69

G
Heikal in **Gaddafi's** clothes —38
"The nice **girl**" —53, 55, 93-95
God is no longer with us —31
Grieve not, for **God** is with us —27, 30
God was, and there was nothing with Him —27
Ibn Taymiyyah, me and **God** face the world —30
The **Green** Shadow —39-40

H
The importance of **hatred** —32-33
Heikal in Gaddafi's clothes —38
#with_neither_despair_nor_**hope** —81-82

I

Ibn Arabi corrects prophet **Ibrahim** —42-43
Ibn Ata'illah abstains —25
Ibn Ata'illah's Aphorisms —26-27
Ibn Taymiyyah, me and God face the world —30
Everyone's against **Ibn Taymiyyah** —28-30
The attendance of the **imagination** —42, 56
Interpretation redeems the world —42-44
There's no such thing as **Israel** —63

J

Jerusalem —54, 57, 58, 60
The liberation of **Jerusalem** begins in Cairo? —58-60

K

Killing the son —39, 42-43, 46
The **killing** of the Council of Senior Scholars —43-44
Milan **Kundera**, *Identity*, 1998 —74

L

The **Labyrinth** —11-13, 17-19, 55, 76, 81
Child in the **labyrinth** —12
The **Latin** dictionary —17
Verses of **Latin** poetry —17
To the **left** —61
The **liberation** of Jerusalem begins in Cairo? —58-60
Love of the sole witness —37-38

M

The destruction of City Stars **Mall** —106
Slipping toward **meaning** —55
The other **memory** —94, 107-108
Broken **microphone** —33
The smile of Abul 'Abbas **al-Mursi** —25
The **Muslim** Brotherhood —58-61, 103-104

N

Ahmed **Naji** —98-99
Fingernails in the neck —94-97
Nietzsche —83

The **non-believers** —39
Their innate "**nonexistence**" —76

P

A **picture** of peasants destroying the railroad tracks to cut off the path of the English occupation forces during the 1919 revolution —100-103
The land-**plane** —68
At the table of the **People's** Convention —38
Peripatetics —52
The true religion that corresponds to sound **philosophy** —17-18, 37
In search of a **poet** —109-110
Verses of Latin **poetry** —17
Preaching in the Sultan Hassan mosque —31-32
The **Presidents'** argument —105
The Citadel **prison** —28
We will return to **prison** sooner or later —88-89

R

The communists and the **red** shadow —40
The true **religion** that corresponds to sound philosophy —17-18, 37
#the_**revolution**_continues —81
No news of the **revolution** on the radio —88
No one does anything outside of the **revolution** —82-83
A picture of peasants destroying the railroad tracks to cut off the path of the English occupation forces during the 1919 **revolution** —100-103
Hannah Arendt, On ***Revolution***, 1963 —81-82
Ruby —100

S

No avoiding **sacrifices** —40
Sartre and Woody Allen in the Friday Sermon —32
The **schism** between will and desire —71
The green **shadow** —39-40
The communists and the red **shadow** —40
The unknown **sister** —13-16
Sisyphus —81
Slipping toward meaning —55
The **smile** of Abul Abbas al-Mursi —25
The existential **smile** —67
The dissolution of **society** —106

Killing the **son** —39, 42-43, 46
Unlicensed **spirit** placation ritual —87
The collapse of the central **state** —106
Street signs in Chinese —62
The **strong** did what they could, and the weak suffered what they must —81
The **Sufis'** intoxication —30-31
The **suppressed** escapes —57

T
Take off your clothes and choose a **task** —98-99
Thanks for the compliment —93-97

V
Verses of Latin poetry —17

W
The strong did what they could, and the **weak** suffered what they must —81
The schism between will and desire —71
Love of the sole witness —37-38
Interpretation redeems the world —42-44

Z
Žižek's barbershop —19
Slavoj **Žižek**, *Welcome to the desert of the real!*, 2002 —19

How to remember your dreams
by Amr Ezzat

This publication is the sixth in the Kayfa ta series. The text was originally authored in Arabic.

Commissioning editors
Maha Maamoun and Ala Younis

Translator
Jennifer Peterson

Design template
Julie Peeters

Cover artwork
Hany Rashed, *Untitled*, from *Maspero Series*, 2006, monoprint (ink on paper), 24 x 18 cm.
Courtesy of the artist

Printers
53dots, Beirut

Publisher
Kayfa ta
www.kayfa-ta.com

ISBN 978-1-955702-04-1

© 2021 Amr Ezzat and Kayfa ta. All rights reserved, including the right of reproduction in whole or in part in any form.

Kayfa ta is an independent publishing initiative founded in 2012.

كيف ت
KAYFA TA